LOVING GOD LOVING OTHERS

Volume 1

A TEN NOWGEN ANTHOLOGY PROJECT

No part of this publication may be reproduced, stored in a retrieval system or transmitted in any form or by any means, electronic, mechanical, photocopying, recording, or otherwise, without express written permission of the authors.

Loving God - Loving Others
A Ten NowGen Anthology Project
Volume I

Copyright © 2025 All rights reserved
ISBN 978-1-949027-11-2

https://ten-worldwide.org
Apostle Katrina Carter
tenteamdirector@tenworldwide.org

Published by:
Destined To Publish | www.DestinedToPublish.com
Flossmoor, Illinois • 773-783-2981

"Train up a child in the way he should go, and when he is old he will not depart from it."
Proverbs 22:6 NKJV

The biblical model of the Kingdom begins at home—with our children. We must be intentional about instilling godly principles early so they have the right foundation to build on as they grow.

The Eagles Network NowGen for children, youth, and teens exists to equip our youngest Kingdom citizens with hope, preparing them to live with purpose and a bright future.

This book is the first installment in **The Good Heart Club series**. It was created in collaboration with Eagles Authors Instructor and publisher Marilyn Alexander, along with her *Destined to Publish* program *Kids Are Authors Too*, which gives young writers the opportunity to develop and publish their stories.

The TEN NowGen Book Project builds on that creativity, inviting children to write through the lens of Kingdom principles. In this volume, students share stories that celebrate loving your neighbor through servanthood, choosing a positive attitude, and knowing that God is our friend whom we talk to through prayer. Each theme connects to what they have learned in **TEN NowGen**, where we believe our children are both the NOW and the future.

In this book, each young author chose from three themes that remind us how we can live out God's love every day. These themes served as a starting point to guide their stories and reflections, and are based on what they are learning in TEN NowGen. The selected themes for this volume are:

- Loving Your Neighbor (Love & Serventhood)
- Being a Good Person (Positive Attitude)
- God Is My Friend (Prayer)

As you read, look for how each writer explored these truths in their own unique way. We hope the stories remind you that these acts create ripples of love that touch everyone around you.

May you always remember that your words, actions, and prayers have the power to inspire others and leave a lasting impact.

Contents

The Good Janitor By Adelais 1

Ely's Big Problem By Alivia 9

I'm God's Soccer Boy by Amadeus 19

Tumbling into Positivity by Imani Grover 29

Love Like God Loves Us by Joel Cheves 47

Ever since he was a baby, Daniel dreamed of outer space. His room was covered head to toe with space-themed wallpapers, lamps, Legos, and even a space-themed pajama set. He was so excited that he even started making rocket models when he was only three years old. Every year for career day, he would dress up as an astronaut and say that he would be the first person to do a triple backflip on the moon.

And now, Daniel couldn't keep his excitement any longer. His science teacher, Mrs. Meyers, had promised them that if the class behaved well enough all year, they would get to go on a field trip to NASA.

Today was that day. His class was well enough behaved all year. Sure, there was the occasional mishap, but well behaved nonetheless. He and his sixth-grade science class were going to NASA!

He had been telling his friends and family about it for weeks. When he finally arrived at school, he was counting down to the very minute until they got to NASA. Two hours, one hour, half an hour. As the NASA sign came into view, Daniel let out a squeal of joy. His dreams from his childhood were finally coming true.

"Now class, stay together. I don't want anybody getting lost or separated from the group," said Mrs. Meyers. As the class walked through the halls led by the head scientist, Daniel noticed his shoes were untied. Remembering what Mrs. Meyers had just said, he yelled for his friends to wait for him, but they were too mesmerized by all the diagrams and technology to listen. Daniel decided that he would catch up after he tied his shoes. Be that as it may, when he looked up, his class was gone. Daniel tried to chase after them, but did they go left instead of right? Or did they stay straight instead of going through that door? He tried to call out for them, but the only noise he heard back was his own echo. Daniel was scared out of his mind.

At long last, Daniel ran into a scientist and tried to ask her for help. The scientist stopped, looked at him confused, checked her watch with a worried look, and said, "Sorry, I'm running late." At that moment, Daniel ran into an engineer, but when he tried to ask for help, the engineer just kept on working and completely took no notice of him. This made him very frustrated as if he could kick the wall, but he decided to push it away.

He wanted to take a break, but in spite of that, he thought it was a good idea to keep moving. He went around asking everyone he could find to help him find his class, but everyone was too "busy" to help. After asking just about everyone he could, he came across a janitor mopping the hallway. He didn't think this janitor could help, but he decided it was worth a shot.

When Daniel went up to the janitor, it took him a while to get his attention because the janitor was blasting some sort of pop-rock music combo from his headphones. After ten tries, Daniel finally got the janitor's attention. With a lot of patience, Daniel explained what had happened, trying to hold back tears. The janitor was still shocked that Daniel wanted to ask him for help.

He knew he needed this hall's mopping to be over and done with, but he thought that he should help Daniel first. "Well, Daniel, you must be very scared right now," the janitor said. "Let me introduce myself. My name is Paul, and welcome to NASA. How about I tell you a story and give you a tour of all you missed?" Daniel nodded his head and smiled. He had missed a lot while running around and didn't mind a story while they walked.

"Let me tell you, Daniel, this is no ordinary story," Paul began. "This is how the king of the world came and saved every single one of us."

Daniel then began to wonder out loud, "A king saved all of us?"

"Yes, Daniel, every single boy and girl." As they passed labs and machinery, Paul then began to explain that Jesus was this king and that he died to pay for all the sins of the world.

"Wait a minute," Daniel interrupted, "this Jesus guy decided to die to save us all from something called sin."

"That's right," answered Paul.

"So then that's it. That's the end of the story." Daniel said, with a frown on his face, confused.

"Of course not." Paul said with a sparkle in his eye and a wide smile. "Jesus's father, named God, brought him back to life." Daniel had heard of God before, but only for special holidays and events some of his friends and family invited him to. "Daniel, do you know that Jesus did this because he wants you to have a relationship with him?" Paul asked. Daniel shook his head. "Do you want to have a relationship with him?"

Daniel paused for a moment and thought over what Paul had told him. "Yes, I would like a relationship with God." Daniel then prayed with Paul to accept Jesus into his heart.

After they were done praying, Daniel asked Paul to tell him more about Jesus. For the rest of the time they spent together, all they did was talk about Jesus and all the cool stuff he did on earth.

As Paul was finishing up the story of how Jesus fed five thousand people, the two finally caught up with Daniel's class. Before Paul officially dropped him off, Paul made Daniel promise to tell others the stories he told Daniel. Daniel promised and joined his friends with a big smile. "Hey guys," he said, "let me tell you a story."

Daniel was in the place of his dreams. He was surrounded by gadgets and gizmos. But during his time at NASA, he found something even better. He found a Savior. He found Jesus.

ABOUT ME

My name is Adelais Palmer, I am 15 years old and I am a sophomore in High School. My favorite subject is chemistry. I like to sing, play instruments, make music, as well as play sports, my favorite being basketball. One of my favorite things we did in this Author's class was in the very beginning. We had made a funny story just by using parts of speech and different random characters we made up. This made me and my peers laugh out loud for a while.

One unique thing I want readers to know about me is that when I was writing this story, The Good Janitor, I had intended to base it off of when John F. Kennedy was visiting NASA and went around asking everyone what their jobs were. All of them answered their generic responses, but when Kennedy asked a janitor, the janitor replied, "I'm sending a man to the moon." One thing I want readers to take away from my story is that you are never too busy to do what's right.

Once upon a time there was a girl named Ely, who was 15 years old. She was very helpful and always had a smile on her face. Her smile stretched from cheek to cheek and brightened every room she entered. Ely also loved to help people.

One day, about five months ago, a shooting star crashed into her backyard. The crash scared Ely out of her sleep. She raced to her backyard and walked closer and closer to the hole in the ground.

In the hole there was a blinding light, so bright that she couldn't see. After it stopped shining, there was a yellow glow, but she didn't know what it was. Even though her mother always told her not to touch strange things, she touched it anyway. It was a crystal.

Ely touched the crystal made out of light, and her entire body began to glow. She wanted to go back to her bedroom, and before she knew it, she was in her room. "Wow, what happened!?" Ely looked around. She said, "I was just in my backyard and now I'm in my room. Did I just teleport?"

Ely thought, "No, I must be tired and I just need to go to bed." Ely flew across the room to her light switch. "No way, did I just fly across the room? I have superpowers!!!" The crystal must have given Ely the powers of flight and teleportation. Ely now had a secret: she was a superhero.

Ely also had a twin sister named Emma. She had not seen her twin sister since they were five years old. She didn't remember much about Emma except that she was unkind, and Ely believed Emma never really cared about her. Ely and Emma's parents separated when they were five because they didn't get along. So, Ely lived with their mother in New York, and Emma lived with their father in Texas.

One day, her twin sister came. Ely was so happy but confused. Emma never came to New York to visit her because it was so far from Texas. Ely went in for a hug and started crying. Ely couldn't believe that Emma was really here. Emma was surprised Ely was crying. Ely said, "I missed you so much, Emma." Emma was mad and pushed her away and yelled, "If you missed me, Ely, you would have visited me!"

Ely said, "I'm sorry, I had to save New York."

"So saving a city is more important than saving me," Emma said.

"No," said Ely, "there's people in need! Don't you get it? Get it through your head. I want to help the kids with special needs. They are too young and can't do things on their own."

Emma said, "I can't believe you. Ever since we were little, you've always put others before me. You always betray me, and that's why I went to live with Daddy."

Emma's words hurt. Ely hadn't known Emma really felt this way. Emma had enough, and she leaped on Ely.

She was so angry. "Hey, get off of me!" Ely said. Emma continued to hit Ely and pushed her away again. "Why are you so mean to me?" Ely said. "Why are you so evil, Emma?"

Emma said, "Don't you think I'm in need too? I have not seen you in ten years!!"

All of a sudden it started to rain. As Ely started to run inside from the rain, Emma put her hands in the air towards Ely and lightning came out. Ely dodged it by using her teleportation powers. She thought, "Does Emma have superpowers too?" Ely yelled, "Are you an evil villain?"

"Of course I am," Emma said, with a smirk on her face.

Ely didn't know, but the same shooting star that gave Ely superpowers had split in two: one landed in her backyard in New York, and another landed in Texas. Emma must have gone through the same process as Ely. Emma also had superpowers.

Emma used her lightning on Ely again! Ely teleported behind Emma. "You are a villain!" Ely said. Then Emma started to attack the town. "No! What are you doing?"

"This town has kept you away from me!" Emma shouted.

"No, Emma," Ely said, "don't destroy the town." Emma didn't listen; she just kept shooting lightning out of her hands. "Okay, okay, okay," Ely said.

"How about this?

We can refresh our lives! We can restart here in New York. There are more people in New York that need to be saved here."

"But will this plan still keep you away from me?" Emma asked. "Do you care about this town more than you care about me?" she asked again. "I swear, if this town keeps you away from me, I am going to destroy it!"

"No!" said Ely.

"What!?" Emma said. "That's what I thought."

Ely was frozen. "Please!" Ely said. "If you're going to destroy the town, destroy me first."

Emma looked at Ely. "No! I can't do that to you," Emma said.

"So you do care about me!" Ely said.

"Of course I do! I love you. God always wants us to tell the truth, right?" Emma said. "Mom and Dad always said that honesty is the best policy.

Let's protect the town together. That way, you can keep the town safe and we can always be together!"

Ely was happy. She went in for another hug. This time, Emma started crying. Ely was so happy that Emma did not push her. She actually hugged her back.

The End.

Moral: Always be a kind person because true love means putting others first, even when it's hard.

ABOUT ME

My name is Alivia, but everyone who loves me calls me Livi. I'm 9 years old and a 4th grader with a sunny personality that helps me make friends with people of all ages. I love math and art, and my favorite colors are purple, pink, and teal and I use them in all my crafts and drawings!

One of my other favorite hobbies is swimming. What I enjoyed most about writing my book was adding all the little details. I hope that readers will learn the lesson I care about most and that is to always be kind to others.

I'M GOD'S SOCCER BOY

TOPIC: GOD IS MY FRIEND

BY AMADEUS

Chapter 1
The Beginning

One day there was a boy named Matthew. He loved to play soccer. He didn't know why, but it just energized him. He never joined the school team—that's because he was a gang banger. One day, he decided to try out for the team. A week later, he made the team because he was the best at the tryouts. But instead of congratulating him, his parents grounded him because they had seen him selling drugs on the street. He slammed the door to his room, thoughts spiraling through his head.

You will never be enough, you have no friends, you only made the team because you were lucky. He was so mad that he threw his chair across the room and it smashed, and his grandma's vase broke. He broke down in tears and wondered, when his mom disciplines him, does she love him? Does anyone really love him? But the next soccer practice would change his life.

CHAPTER 2
Angel Jones

I got up in the morning and heard yelling between my mom and my dad. My younger sibling died of cancer two years ago, so ever since, they have been arguing everyday. I did my workout, and then my mom gave me a pep talk about how I need to stop selling drugs and do my chores. I rolled my eyes and she gave me a look like "I don't want to see that again."

Then I went to school ready to bully that one short kid, but I slipped on a leaf, and I got mad and kicked the leaf 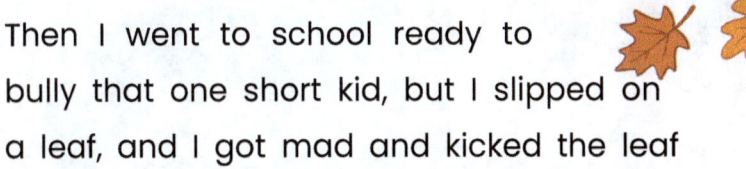 away. It flew into the sky like nothing happened, so I kept going to school. When I got there, the football coach and the team were disappointed that I chose soccer over football, so the captain of the football team shoved me into a locker. I went to tell the soccer coach that I had made a wrong choice, but then I saw a name below mine on the roster that I hadn't seen yesterday: Angel.

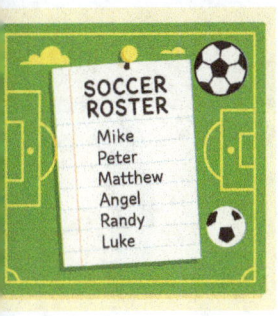

Then some new student came rushing through the hall looking for me. He looked Asian and of average height, with one green eye and one brown eye. "What a weird-looking kid," I thought. "Who decided to have this kid?"

"Hey, my name is Angel Jones." This was Angel Jones?

CHAPTER 3
Introductions and Soccer Practice

"What do you want from me, weird-looking kid?" I said.

Angel replied, "I just want to congratulate you on being the best player at tryouts, mate!"

"First of all, it was just luck. Second, why are you so nice?"

Angel replied, "First, I think that was raw talent that you were showing on the field yesterday. Second, mate, I think that's what God called us to do."

"Wait, you think God is real? And why are you talking in a British accent?"

Angel replied, "Yes, God does exist."

I interrupted him, "God is not real, but anyway, continue."

"Ooooookayyyy. And my accent is because I'm British, Korean, and American."

"Ugh. This is gonna be a long soccer year," I said, rolling my eyes. "I think I may go do football instead."

Angel said, "No, you're too good not to play soccer."

I remembered that at soccer practice, Angel was bugging the coach if he could do something, but what was it? When she finally agreed, Angel started speaking about God, and to my surprise, the others were interested except for me. Later, Angel and I had a talk about what he said at practice, and I had a lot of questions. He was so surprised he almost popped his eyes out of his own head. Then I went home and my family asked, "How was practice today?" I said it was fine and went to bed.

Chapter 4

Today when I woke up, I surprisingly heard my parents talking. No yelling, no arguing, just talking. When I asked them what they were talking about, they said, "Oh, we are thinking about going to church." Those were the two words that Angel said yesterday, church and God, so I quickly ran to school, and for once, I was actually happy. I didn't even slip on any leaves, and I chose right instead of wrong that day. I saw Angel and told him what my mom told me, and he was overjoyed that I was overjoyed. "Dude, this is amazing, you get to be with people who love God."

Angel and I were giggling and laughing all day, so we had to get detention for two days. That was the shortest detention I've ever had. I felt so lucky, I asked my mom if we could go to Angel's church and she said yes. Then at church, I gave my life to Christ for the first time. And that changed my life forever. I thank Jesus for him being my friend through the tough times and for guiding me to you.

DETENTION SLIP
Name: Angel
Reason: Disruptive in class (giggling and laughing)

DETENTION SLIP
Name: Matthew
Reason: Disruptive in class (giggling and laughing)

My name is Amadeus. I am 11 years old. I am in 6th grade and my favorite subject is reading. I like to play soccer outside of school.

I loved being creative when I was writing my story. I hope the lesson you get from my story is that God is our friend.

Did you know gymnastics is the most popular sport in the Summer Olympics? From flips to splits, gymnastics allows your side of life to be shown. Gymnastics is a great sport to show your athletic and powerful side on vault, your personality and creativity side on floor, your resilience and capability side on bars, and your confidence and focused side on beam. 🖤 Gymnastics is a great way to have fun and express yourself because it combines athletics and dance. Gymnastics also builds character, discipline, working hard, and believing in your abilities.

My Background

🖤Hi, my name is Aria J., but my friend calls me Ari, and I love to dance. Dancing is movement flowing through your body to express yourself with or without music. I always have a rhythm rippling through my body like a flowing river. That's why the floor exercise is my favorite gymnastics event.

Being able to shine in the spotlight and moving to a rhythm makes me feel like I belong.

My rich dark brown wavy hair is usually tucked back in a bubble braid or a messy bun, secured down with two hair clips for the front two pieces. My brown hazel eyes shine in the spotlight when I leap across the floor and move to the music. My skin color is like maple syrup glazing on pancakes or waffles. The way these foods make you feel good and are warm on the inside, that's my personality. I feel good when I share my positivity with others.

When the Struggle Gets Real

It can be hard to be positive, supportive, and your true self if you hear your teammates talking behind your back or talking about your skill level. Hearing your teammates talking behind your back negatively will probably make you doubt yourself, make you feel disappointed, and make you feel like you're not good enough. This usually happens if you are new. You might be excluded or picked on, and you might feel like you don't belong or are the odd one out. This also usually happens if someone is jealous. They might pick on you and bully you about your appearance, how you act, how you do things in life, or what you like to do. This behavior hurts, and it doesn't feel good to be judged.

A Fresh Start

When I was walking into my new gymnastics gym, Northville Gymnastics Center, I was really excited to try something new and meet new people. When I walked in, I felt a wave of chilly air. It seemed about 65 degrees in the lobby. The lobby had "NGC" in all caps with orange, white, and black stripes crisscrossing on the walls. The chairs were black with orange and white stars on them, and "NGC" was in the middle. On one of the walls, there was a TV that  had cameras of what I thought was inside of the gym. I didn't see any gymnasts or coaches on the cameras; it was probably a REC team or the beginner, intermediate, and advanced levels.

After I took off my pink and white Converse and my gray hoodie that has "love others" on the back in black and matching black leggings that have "love others" in gray down the side, I waited in the lobby in one of the chairs. I knew this was going to be a great experience and a fun summer. Then I heard two voices talking, so I followed where the voices were coming from, because I didn't know where the gym was or how to get there. The door was slightly open and some light came through the small opening.

Inside, there was a young woman who looked around 20 and had a name tag that said "Coach Brianna." She had slightly brownish-tan skin and curly hair that went just past her elbow. Her brown hair with highlights was pulled back in a high ponytail with the front two pieces curling in the front. Her eyes were dim brown like autumn leaves. She had baby pink nails that had bows and polka dots on them, clear glasses that didn't have any filth in the lenses, and large gold hoops that had a twist detail on them. She was wearing an orange shirt that said "NGC" on the front in all caps outlined in black and had white stars scattered all around the shirt. On the back, it said "Coach Brianna." She had black leggings that had "happy" on the side in pink and black sneakers with a hint of white.

There was also a young man who looked around 25 and had a name tag that said "Coach Drew." He had a black shirt that said "NGC" outlined in orange and had white stars on it and had "Coach Drew" on the back. He had light tan skin and fluffy tan hair with the slightest little waves, with a hint of brow,. and light brown eyes that looked like honey glaze. He wore orange shorts that came down to his knees and had white shoes.

When I walked in, the coaches smiled and introduced themselves. "Hi, and welcome. My name is Coach Brianna, and I'll be here most days except Wednesday.

I'll help you meet all the girls. For the first two or three weeks, the other girls are going to wear their leotards that have their first name and last initial on them and a fun fact about them."

"Welcome to NGC. My name is Coach Drew and I'll be here every other day, I'll help you know where everything is like equipment, the bathroom, and where to find the gym."

Then Coach Brianna told me to rotate to the window and said, "In the gym we have our REC in the front, which is our younger gymnasts that are five and below. There's the beam, rings, tunnel, and mini foam pit. We also have our beginner, intermediate, and advanced classes slightly further back. Then there are the team events, where you will be having practice this summer."

Soon after Coach Brianna finished talking, Coach Drew told me, "We have an orange schedule board in the back and a calendar board by the bars. The schedule board will tell you what group you're in, when you rotate to your next event or break, and the calendar board tells you when we have meet season, when we don't have practice, when we have special practices, which is when Thanksgiving and Christmas come and we decorate the gym, and when we have showcases. Showcases are when everyone shows skills on each event to the team and the team votes on who is the best in their groups. The winner after each gets three prizes from the orange bin by the floor."

Coach Brianna also told me that we had two other coaches in the gym, Coach Makayla and Coach Elliot. She said, "Coach Makayla will help you learn all the routines on all the events, and she will be here every day." In the window, there was a caramel brown young woman with long brown knotless braids that reached her lower back. She was wearing an orange zip-up baggy sweatshirt that had "NGC" in the top corner in black, and she had black leggings. She was wearing white Adidas shoes with pink laces.

On the floor by a group of girls, there was a light caramel young man wearing a name tag that had "Coach Elliot" on it. He had on a white long-sleeved T-shirt with "NGC" in orange and black stars all around the shirt. He had black baggy pants, white socks, and white shoes. He had tan wavy hair with hints of blond in it. Coach Elliot's hair kind of looked like Coach Drew's, and Coach Brianna kind of looked like Coach Makayla. I wondered if they were siblings. Coach Brianna said, "Coach Elliot is our health and wellness expert. He focuses on healthy eating and mental toughness. He will be here every Monday, Tuesday, and Thursday."

Is it just me, or did it seem like they were practicing their "speech" for a couple of hours? 😊 😊 The coaches seemed warm, friendly, and kind. They made me feel even more excited about going to the gym. The T-shirts and hoodies they wore were something I hoped to get one day. The coaches looked proud and confident that I really wanted to be a part of this team.

When I walked into the gym with the coaches, there were 10-15 other girls sitting on the spring floor. Each girl was wearing matching leos that were half  orange, black, and white that criss-crossed and had

"NGC" in the middle like the walls in the lobby, and the rest was black. On the back of the leotard, it said their names, and under that was their fun fact. I could really stand out. I was wearing a bright pink leotard that had lemons on it, and the rest of the team had orange, black, and white leotards.

As I got close, I could already feel the cold stares from some of the other gymnasts. Not all seemed to be bugged or disturbed by me; some waved, and some gave a thumbs-up. I felt a little bit better because of those friendly acknowledgments. I tried to smile and wave at a few of them to show that I was nice, but some stared harder or looked away. I didn't feel like I belonged, and I did feel like the odd one out. I didn't even have a matching leotard. 😊 I thought to myself, "Don't try to fit in if you were born to stand out." I kept repeating it in my head until I believed in myself. I know that being yourself is the best way for me to stay happy.

Even though I was trying to stay positive, I wasn't even welcomed by some of the other gymnasts. 😊 One girl gave me the side-eye that was so deep it made my stomach flip-flop into a somersault. I looked on the back of her leotard and saw that her name was Calia

S. Calia had strawberry tan hair that was braided down her back. It kind of looked like Rapunzel, but it wasn't dragging on the floor. Her skin tone reminded me of dry and wet sand mixed together. She has hazel eyes that shimmered whenever she did a skill well. Calia loved bars, not just because she was good at them, but because she liked to flip high. I knew this because that's what I heard from a group of girls sitting near me. It was also on the back of her leotard as her fun fact.

Shoved, Snatched, and Sprayed

Calia seemed like she wanted me to feel uncomfortable or she wanted me to feel that she was better than me. I felt very small and alone. No one wanted to talk to me, so I talked to Coach Makayla. She said, "I love your leotard. The colors are bright and look pretty with each other." I knew that Coach Makayla was there for me. Still, I felt everyone was looking at me during warm-up and stretching. There were some glances and stares that were kind of intimidating. I knew I had to do my best always and show them that I had skills.

At first, it seemed like we were going to get along, until, when we went to the bars and I was getting my chalk, Calia shoved me out of the way. This made me topple over on my own feet. I got so confused. Was this a mistake? Maybe? Maybe not? Then Calia stole the spray bottle right out of my hand like I wasn't even holding it. I was surprised. Then she sprayed water in my face. I was trying to brush this off, but I got the three-piece combo—shoved, snatched, and sprayed. At first, I was bothered, but then I realized that the water on my face was actually refreshing.

The Power of Positivity

As soon as Calia put the spray bottle back on the holder, I grabbed the bottle and rubbed chalk on my grips, and I quickly walked past her so I could do my routine. I felt slightly embarrassed because I had toppled over my feet, turned them into a pretzel, and almost fallen down, but I was determined to do my best. When I got to the bars, I remembered Galatians 5:22-23, which reads:

But the fruit of the Spirit is love, joy, peace, patience, kindness, goodness, faithfulness, gentleness, and self-control. Against such things there is no law.

That's the New English Translation. My favorite! I know that living by the fruits of the Spirit will make an impact, and it calms me down. I took a few deep breaths before I started my routine. The gym was silent. I felt all eyes on me. I knew the other gymnasts would want to see how good of a gymnast I was, and that's probably why they were all staring at my every move.

When I was going for the dismount, out of nowhere Caila coughed very loud, which broke my concentration and focus. I saw some girls give a thumbs-up—they probably noticed that Caila was trying to make me mess up. I almost flung myself off the bar, but I still went for the dismount. I swung harder; I knew I had to show the other gymnasts and Calia how good I was. I was determined to land the dismount, so I went for it and

I landed it. Not perfect. I wobbled a little and took a tiny step. But it was somewhat good. I was feeling courageous, strong, and good inside after I landed that dismount because I did it with Calia's fake coughing. The other girls started to break out into conversation. They were probably talking about my routine, things that were good and things that were bad about it.

Finding a Solution

Sometimes it can be hard to hear others talking about you. Some ways to not have your teammates talking about you or your skills are to be positive, cheerful, and supportive all the time, especially to the person or people who are picking on you or talking about you. Getting bullied, it can be hard to stay calm and peaceful when they are calling you names and teasing you. If you're being compassionate and considerate to others, no one should talk negatively about you. You can also introduce yourself if you haven't told your teammates some hobbiaes and some facts about yourself. Telling your teammates some facts about yourself like your favorite food, color, and what you like to do in your free time can make them feel more comfortable around you.

During break time, I decided to introduce myself to a group of girls. Some of the girls were the ones who smiled at me when I came in the gym and some were not, but they still seemed nice. I introduced myself and told them how I loved to dance and that the floor was my favorite event. I asked the girls about their fun facts on the back of their leotards.

After that, they wanted to know what gym I transferred from. I told them that I was originally from Elite Allstars Gymnastics. It seemed like we were all going to be close friends. I was slightly nervous to ask them about Calia because I did just get shoved, sprayed, and snatched like 20 minutes ago. But I asked them if Calia was mean to them too. They said, "Kinda. But don't worry about it, you'll get used to it sooner or later. Eventually, she'll stop picking on you. Once she sees you have skills, she will start being there for you."

Another way to stop being picked on is to talk to an adult, like your parents, coaches, or a trusted person who is 18 or older. You should tell them about how some of your teammates have been picking on you and treating you unpleasantly at practice. They can contact the gym about the problem. This can work because they hear both sides of the problem and can help make a good solution.

Staying kind, staying true to yourself, and asking for help can make all the difference.

After we finished floor and beam, our last two events, I waited in the lobby for my mom to come pick me up. I FaceTimed on the phone with Jiselle, a family friend, about the situation while I was waiting. Jiselle said, "Since you're new, your teammates might be different around you because they don't know you very much. You should talk to your parents about it and see if they can talk to the coaches about the situation." Jiselle liked that I introduced myself to a group of girls on the team. She said, "The more people you know, the less people will act differently around you." After the conversation with Jiselle, I felt like I had a better approach to this situation. I knew what I had to do next to resolve this conflict.

I was a little nervous, but I talked to my parents about how Calia had been treating me that day and how some of the other gymnasts greeted me poorly. Then I told them, "Jiselle wanted me to tell you that the coaches were nice to me, but it would be great if they could have introduced me better with a game like 'Would you rather?'"

My parents FaceTimed with Coaches and told them how Calia tried to mess me up on the bars and what she did with the chalk and spray bottle. Coach Brianna was surprised to hear that Calia had a "lack of kindness." She said that she would talk to Calia. Coach Mikayla said that she would create a fun game like "Simon Says Gymnastics" to help the girls get to know me.

After a day or two, things started to feel more welcoming. We played more introductory games for warm-up. I felt better and still tried to be nice to Calia. We weren't the best of friends, but Calia didn't give me more trouble. On Wednesday, Coach Makayla gave me an orange zip-up baggy sweatshirt that matched hers, but on the back, it had "Gymnast Aria."

What I Learned

Life often throws obstacles, but obstacles don't have to stay obstacles. Having a positive attitude helps with the way you respond to problems. I've learned to work around them and make a positive outcome. I've also learned that being positive isn't always easy, but it's the only way to make things better.

Every time I felt like giving up, I remembered how hard I worked to get here. I realized that no matter how others treat me, I have the power to choose how I respond. By being kind, staying true to myself, and not letting the negativity bring me down, I've learned that I can achieve anything I set my mind to. I know now that being positive can help fix problems. From now on, I know that being positive will take me farther than I ever thought possible.

My name is Imani, and I am 10 years old. My name means "faith" in Swahili. I love gymnastics, watching videos, and creating things through different forms of art. I'm in 5th grade, and my favorite subjects in school are writing and art.

One of my favorite parts of the Authors Class was how Ms. Marilyn taught us. She made us laugh, and she showed us a roller coaster at the beginning of class to explain how every story should have both good and bad parts.

Overall I loved this class and it was a great experience! The message I hope students would take away from my story is that life often has obstacles but there's always a way to find a positive outcome when life is hard.

Love Like God Loves Us

Theme: Loving Your Neighbor

By Joel

There was once a boy who had just moved back to his hometown after nine years. His name was James. He lived near the church, and he also loved the youth group. Most of his old friends still lived in the same small, quiet town, and they all hung out every weekend. He was building a better relationship with them, now more than ever.

Now, James and his friends loved playing sports, but the most important sport that they liked was volleyball. They played it more than any other sport! They went to the park and got a net and they started playing volleyball, but all of a sudden, they heard a truck with loud music and they went to it. James had a feeling that it was not going to end well. James and his friends went, riding their bikes, following the truck to a sold house. James was wrong. He thought that something bad was going to happen. So many things were going through his head: kidnapping, drugging, and many more possibilities.

James and his friends went closer to the truck. As they got closer, James saw a lot of faces. James started to realize that he had new neighbors! He told his friends that they just moved here and they needed to introduce themselves. His friends said that they just wanted to go back to the park. James got really mad, even furious. Yelling at his friends, he started to bike home.

A couple days passed. James kept on thinking about the new neighbors and how he and his friends were so rude, and also how he got angry and furious and just left. Now, there is a little thing to know about James. He is a happy soul and he knows how to have a positive attitude in bad situations, but he had discernment.

James decided to go bike to the new neighbors house. He didn't know if they were home, so he rang the doorbell. A young girl with brown hair and dark green eyes answered the door and acted surprised. James started saying, "Hello, my name is James Hamilton. I live about seven houses from here. My friends and I were in front of your house when you drove in, and I just wanted to say sorry for the disrespectfulness and the rudeness that we gave you guys by not introducing ourselves. What's your name?" The girl at the door

suddenly answered saying, "My name is Ester."

"That is a beautiful name," James said, filled with surprise. James didn't know how to feel, he felt so many emotions.

Ester closed the door, saying, "It has been a pleasure talking to you. Have a wonderful day!"

After Ester closed the door, James rode his bike back home. James never expected that God would teach him something so real through a cardboard box and a girl next door. The first time he saw Ester, she was lifting boxes from the back of a moving van, her curls tied in a loose bun, her arms full of books and lamps. It wasn't dramatic—no glowing light or angel chorus—but something stirred quietly in James's heart. She was his *neighbor* now. And suddenly, a Bible verse he'd heard his whole life felt more than just words: *"Love your*

Love your neighbor as yourself.

Mark 12:31

neighbor as yourself" (Mark 12:31). It stuck with him all week.

He thought about it during youth groups, during math class, even while taking out the trash. *God,* he prayed one evening, *what does that really mean—to love your neighbor?* He kept asking until he felt the answer settle deep in his heart: *"It means noticing. Inviting. Listening. Opening the door."* So James did something simple, something that felt a little scary: He invited Ester to a youth group. And she came. Week after week, they walked to church together. They talked about God, life, family, and music. Ester asked good questions— sometimes hard ones. But she was searching, and James could tell God was gently working on her heart.

One Friday afternoon, with summer heat warming the sidewalks, James felt a nudge again. *Invite her over.* Not for anything big—just a casual visit. A movie. A few laughs. An open door. He hesitated. Would she think it was weird? Too much? But then he remembered—*love isn't about perfect timing. It's about showing up.* So as they walked home from school, he took a breath and asked. "Hey, want to come over tomorrow? We could hang out, watch something, and I'll show you my terrible garage drum set." Ester laughed. "Sure. That sounds fun." The next day, she came over. They talked more than they watched the movie, and somewhere between the popcorn and the half-smashed bucket drums, Ester looked around and said softly, "It feels different here. Peaceful." James glanced at her. "Like... I don't know," she continued. "Like God's real here. I've been trying to figure out if I even believe in Him. But being around you... your family... it makes me wonder."

James didn't say anything right away. He felt that same quiet awe from weeks ago. The sense that God was doing something much bigger than he could see. All he had done was invite. Open a door. Be a friend. And in doing so, he had obeyed something holy: *"Love your neighbor."* Not with grand speeches, but with popcorn. With walks to church. With patience, kindness, and presence. James smiled. "Maybe that's God's way of showing you He's real—through small things."

Ester nodded. "If that's true... then it's kind of a miracle, isn't it?"

James looked at her, heart full. "Yeah. It really is."

A couple days passed. On a cool Sunday morning at Peace Creek Church, worship was starting, and James was hanging out with some of the youth. When worship started, James and some youth ran to the front, but James forgot one thing, "Ester!!!" James excitedly said. Ester was wearing a dress full of colorful  flowers and flowered high heels, weirdly matching with James. Ester was happy to see James. Likewise with James. They sat next to each other during the service. After the service, they went to go eat with both of their families, and James and Ester said their goodbyes.

Lying in bed, all of a sudden James had a dream. In this dream, he was to marry Ester, and this was very clear.

"James, you are a faithful and obedient servant of the Lord. When I told you to love your neighbor as yourself, you obeyed and did not question—scared, yes, but you did it anyway. You are my son, and I love you in and out." That was very clear to James.

The next day, James saw Ester and ran outside. Ester was happy, but she had bad news and didn't know how to say it. James asked her what was wrong. Ester explained, " James, I don't know how to say this, but I'm moving."

James stared at her, confused. James started tearing up, but he didn't want to show weakness. A voice spoke to James saying, "It's okay, you need it."

James started crying, and Ester started holding him and hugging him. "It's okay, I'm here," Ester said peacefully. She and James talked and said their goodbyes.

Every day since then, James has been thinking about Ester. One day, James gets a call from an unknown person, picks it up, and hears a female voice.

It's Ester.

ABOUT ME

My name is Joel. I am 15 years old and I'm in 10th grade. My favorite hobbies are playing volleyball and making music. My favorite subject isn school is math (so good). My biggest dream is to make my music so big so that everyone can hear it.

My favorite part of the the authors class is when we started writing our stories. One hope I have for the readers of my story is to love like God loves us. Love our friends, our neighbors, our family, our Lord. My story demonstrates this, love like God loves us.

Dr. Pamela Scott is a pioneer and reformer in the worship arts. While dancing on Broadway, she encountered Jesus and soon began serving the nations as an evangelist and as Director of the International Dance Fellowship (1984–1988). Since then, she has ministered in more than 35 nations.

In 2008, God gave Apostle Pamela Scott, Founder of EITI and TEN Worldwide, the vision for The Eagles Network (TEN) Worldwide. Its first graduating class included 175 students, and today TEN graduates more than 500 students annually in over 30 nations.

TEN Worldwide provides a full range of equipping courses for ministers serving in the Kingdom Arts. These clusters align directly with the accredited Apostolic

Training Center and College, Eagles International Training Institute (EITI).

Through her pioneering leadership, Dr. Scott continues to impact nations by raising up ministers, reformers, and leaders who use their gifts in worship and the arts to advance the Kingdom of God.

Apostle Katrina R. Carter is a wife, mother, and international leader who was called to ministry in 2007 after a life-changing encounter with the Lord at a fountain in Eden Park, Cincinnati, Ohio. From that moment, her path was radically transformed.

She began her ministry journey through dance, preaching, teaching, and evangelism. Today, she is most notably recognized for her service as an equipper in the prophetic and in the ministry of the supernatural power of God.

A natural leader, Apostle Katrina has served faithfully in both marketplace and ministry roles. She is the founder of Heavenly Dove Ministries (2014) and has served as Director of The Eagles Network (TEN) Worldwide since 2016, where she continues to impact lives globally through training, equipping, and empowering others to walk in their God-given purpose.

In the marketplace, she has served in Early Childhood Education as a teacher, leader, coach, trainer, and community liaison since 2008. She believes all children can learn and deserve equitable opportunities for success, regardless of background or developmental needs.

www.ingramcontent.com/pod-product-compliance
Lightning Source LLC
LaVergne TN
LVHW021717080426
835510LV00010B/1012